RACISM

And

WHITE FRAGILITY

"Combating Racism and Teaching Race Consciousness."

By
Barry Foster

This document is geared towards providing exact and reliable information about the topic and issue covered. The publication is sold with the idea that the publisher is not required to render accounting, officially permitted or otherwise qualified services. If advice is necessary, legal or professional, a practiced individual in the profession should be ordered.

- From a Declaration of Principles which was accepted and approved equally by a Committee of the American Bar Association and a Committee of Publishers and Associations.

The information provided herein is stated to be truthful and consistent, in that any liability, in terms of inattention or otherwise, by any usage or abuse of any policies, processes, or directions contained within is the sole and utter responsibility of the recipient reader. Under no

TABLE OF CONTENTS

WHAT IS RACISM

The first step to ending racism is to understand what it really is. It is going to be easy, though. If you are not sure what racism is, and how it looks, then that is all right. This book can serve as a helpful guide; we put it together to help you identify and avoid racism.

When anyone asks me where I first encounter racism, I will insist on any stage of the school system, from nursery upwards. It is here where children know about other cultures. This is where racism can begin. Racism is about three issues to me: greed, wealth, and terror. Second, it is about moving over and modifying every single part of another race.

The picture is bigger than this. People use racism to make money. Through racism, people keep other people down. People can brainwash and trick mainly poor people into fighting each other. We do not get to fight each other anywhere. The question is the framework, which in the first place makes us thought this way.

Origins of Racism

We are all getting used to the word racism. It is noticed on television, the highway, at work, at college, etc. There has been a substantial period where the notion of racism included that certain citizens may be viewed poorly, put down, mocked, or threatened merely because of the society from which they are descended. For many, the use of racism revolves around the color of one's skin. However, there have not always been the same attitudes towards people of different cultural origins.

Transatlantic slavery has played a crucial role in the development and dissemination of racial ideas. By reflecting on how racism came in and how it improved, we will try to grasp it and then feel better prepared to cope with it.

DEFINITIONS OF RACISM

First, do we all have the same definition of what we call 'racism'? There is a great deal of confusion about what that word means. Some people say that someone could act in a racist manner because of ignorance. Others say that racist people are being persuaded by others or copying other behavior. However, none of this tells us how racism began, and if we can get to the root cause.

Is racism the same thing as racial racism? Can anyone be racist? The response is not obvious. Human beings have always had racism against other people who might come from another area or country. People will often say this is racist. There are, though, different views on what is specifically racist. Racism is, in simple terms, the belief that there are distinct human races and that one race is superior to another. Oxford English Dictionary, Merriam-Webster Dictionary (U.S.A.), and the Macquarie Dictionary (Australia) generally agree to this definition.

One common view is that racism and racial racism are the same things. Basing thoughts and feelings on people off their cultural and national origins means that anyone can be racist to another person. Racism simply goes both ways among any race that has conflict. This sense of racism often comes to mind when a lot of people use derogatory words against another culture. It also ignores the ways in which one race can suppress and exploit another race, like transatlantic slavery.

Racism is the assumption that one human race is superior to another. The intrinsic biological features of a person predetermine the social and moral features of the human. Ethnic separatism is the idea that distinct races, which often adheres to racism, should remain independent and segregated from each other. It can be identified by another as one's hate — or the conviction that another person is less than perfect — because of the color of the skin, language, traditions, place of birth, or some aspect that supposedly exposes the person's basic existence. This has been a common theme throughout human history. It has shaped battles, colonialism, nation-building, and legal codes.

In the last 500 to 1000 years, racism by the western powers towards non-westerners has had a much greater impact on culture than any other type of prejudice (for example, racialism against western or eastern cultures such as Asians, Africans, etc.).Western slavery has been the most infamous form of colonialism. This is particularly true for the enslavement of Africans in the Modern World (slavery itself goes back thousands of years). This enslavement was accomplished due to the racist conviction that Black Africans were less fully human than white Europeans and their descendants.

This belief was not "automatic". The idea of Africans being inferior to colonists was one that is consider slow forming. When Portuguese sailors first visited Africa in the fifteenth and sixteenth centuries, they came to colonies and towns as developed as their own and treated Africans as significant rivals. Over time, however, when African cultures struggled to meet Europe's technical advancements, this began the notion of Europe's extreme superiority. Major European powers started plundering the continent and forcefully extracting its people to serve within new colonies throughout the Atlantic. Thus, creating the mindset that Africans were a poor "race" or better yet, "savages." Some Africans desired to earn profits by selling other Africans to European slave dealers, which contributed to savagery arguments. There were centered on the mistaken assumption that the "black people" were all kinsmen, all members of one society — as compared to several separate, often warring countries.

One significant feature of racism, especially towards Africans and immigrant communities, is its stance towards slaves and slavery. Anti-Semites generally see Jews as subhuman but also superhuman: devilishly clever, skillful, and strong. Racists regard people of ethnicity as pure subhuman, almost like beasts rather than people. If the basis of anti-Semitism is evil, the basis of racism is inferiority — aimed at those who were often perceived to lack even the capacity to be bad.

Throughout the second half of the 19th century, Darwinism was a challenge to their spiritual hegemony by many White westerners, the loss in Christian identity, and increasing immigration. European thinkers and philosophers, and to a lesser degree U.S. scholars, formulated fake racial intelligence to justify non-Jewish white supremacy. While much of these ostensibly empirical attempts to elevate one race over another, they were debunked by the Nazi annihilation of Jews. A limited number of scientists and social science continued to contend in the 20th century about the inborn defects of other races, especially those of African American descent. At the same moment, certain public figures in the African American community promoted their own race's supremacy and racial inferiority-using almost the same white racist terminology.

All these statements are based on the false understanding of race. In fact, there is no agreement among contemporary scientists about whether race is a valid way of classifying people. There is no scientific significance of what some people consider to be major "cultural" variations — skin color, hair, facial structure. Indeed, genetic differences within a so-called race may be wider than those between races. One philosopher writes:

> *There are few genetic attributes to be found in the population of England that are not found in similar proportions in Zaire or China .... those differences that affect us most deeply in our dealings with each other are not biologically determined at any significant degree.*

How Do Racial Attitudes Form?

The writer describes the stages of racial perceptions in children as they grow. An infant is conscious of variations in color by age two. The child starts identifying with his or her own racial group within the next two to four years. At that point, the basis of the dominant mindset form with the community and not by interaction with a culturally specific party. Children begin to develop preference patterns. Parents are the earliest and most powerful source of (positive or negative) racial attitudes, while peers are running a close second. Every child carries at least some stereotyping through its early grades.

Institutional and cultural racisms are more subtle in that they are embedded in unexamined assumptions and established practices. These roots are multigenerational and can continue even after years of legislative remedies. The self-depreciation, poor rates of school achievement or general standard of life for citizens of ethnicity have not yet been overcome after a quarter-century since desegregation. Racism in any measure undermines the self-esteem of children and erodes the process of education.

How Extensive Is Racism in Public Schools?

Research revealed that racism persists and could be on the rise in the increasingly moderate, predominantly Caucasian population of Eugene, Oregon. The report emphasized the frequency of racial jokes and slurs, derogatory racial stereotyping and (less often) violent acts that school authorities left unpunished. Augustine Garcia notes that our inner cities and high-density immigration areas (California, Florida) are experiencing Neo-Nazi skinheads and racial gangs intimidating, plus irrational violence. Children from families with dysfunctions are especially vulnerable to social pressure to take a discriminatory stance.

When looking at incidents of racism, it is not just the condescension and violence exhibited towards minorities that must be considered. Restrictions on the chance of minorities succeeding are often determined racially. Asian-Americans, for example, are resenting academic excellence and "overachieving." If Racism is explicit in society's street level, it is often implicit and equally entrenched at the highest levels.

RACISM AND POWER

The significant alternate perspective is that anyone can be racist towards someone else. Conduct like this may be racist even when it comes from the 'race' which, over the years, has become dominant and uses its influence to decrease and improve racism. Many argued that this means that racism is equal to racial racism plus power. Due to this interpretation, while an African American individual might be racist on the grounds of ethnicity against a white person, sometimes aggressively and unjustly. This may not be purely racist since the African American person may not have the perceived protection of agencies like the police or the media behind them. The theory of racism means there are several sections of society and the big institutions operating it, which promote racism, and they endorse what has been proclaimed to be the 'superior' race.

ENTRENCHED INEQUALITIES

Racism can also be found in different social environments. African American children were three times more likely than white children to be excluded permanently from school in 2006, with five or more GCSEs being least likely. The police stop and search African Americans eight times more than white people, and when judged by a judiciary court, they are more likely to be found guilty. Ethnic minorities are more likely to suffer violence and racially biased assaults. Statistics show that African Americans are three times less likely than Caucasians with similar skills to get out of work. They are often subjected to prejudice and intimidation by labor tribunals daily at work.

RACISM THROUGHOUT HISTORY

12.5 million slaves were captured from Africa between 1525 and 1866. Many were shipped to the Americas by the transatlantic slave trade. Any 3.9 million of the 10.7 million people who endured the terrifying two-month journey were slaves in the United States upon entering the Modern World. Understanding the scale of this forced displacement – and the continued dissemination of slavery by intergovernmental commerce around the World – may be an overwhelming challenge, however as Historian Leslie Harris said earlier this year to Amy Crawford from Smithsonian, "the great conceptions of human experience will help explain what this entails."

Take, for example, the John Casor story. Originally an indentured servant of African origin, Casor lost a legal case that was held in 1654 to decide whether his time as an indentured servant had ended. He was the first man in the United States to be declared a slave for life. Manuel Vidau, a Yoruba man, kidnapped and sold to merchants about 200 years after Casor's enslavement. He later exchanged an account of his experience with the British and International Anti-Slavery Movement – after a decade of enslavement in Cuba, he purchased a lottery ticket share and received enough money to purchase his freedom.

Finally, consider the life of the last known transatlantic slave trade survivor, Matilda McCreary. Kidnapped from West Africa and brought to the United States on the Clotilda, she arrived in July 1860 in Mobile, Alabama. This was more than 50 years after Congress had outlawed the importation of enslaved labor. McCrear, who died in 1940, "showed a determined, even defiant streak" in her later life, Brigit Katz wrote earlier this year. She declined to use the last name of her former husband, kept her typical Yoruba-style hair, and had a decades-long relationship with a White German man.

How the horrors of slavery are remembered and taught by American society is crucial. As new research emerges it has been made known that many textbooks offer a balanced interpretation of the past of African American pioneers like Harriet Tubman and Frederik Douglass. The narrative is 'good.' Before 2018, Texas schools have learned that the primary factors of the Civil War were the interests of states and sectionalism — not slavery. Historian Kevin M. Levin writes in Confederate memorials across the country, enslaved individuals are often misrepresented as loyal slaves. Accurately representing slavery could require an updated vocabulary, historian Michael Landis argued in 2015:

Outdated terms such as 'compromise' or 'plantation' served either to reassure worried Americans in a Cold War world, or to uphold a white supremacist, sexist interpretation of the past. Rather than referring to the 1850 Compromise, call it the 1850 Appeasement — a term that better describes the 1850 Compromise.

Smithsonian scholar Christopher Wilson also wrote that the widespread framing of the Civil War as a struggle between equal entities gives legitimacy to the Confederacy, which was not a nation in its own right, but an 'illegitimate rebellion and unrecognized political entity.'

To better understand the immense brutality ingrained in the daily lives of enslaved persons, read up on the Whitney Plantation Museum in Louisiana, which acts as a "part reminder of the scars of institutional bondage, part mausoleum for dozens of enslaved persons who worked (and died) in [its] sugar fields, ... [and] a monument to the terror of slavery," as Jared Keller observed in 2016. Visitors continue their tour in a historic church filled with clay statues of children who died on the property of the plantation, then travel on to a collection of granite slabs inscribed with the names of hundreds of enslaved African Americans. Scattered throughout the experience are stories of the violence that supervisors inflict.

Whitney Plantation Museum is at the center of a heritage site seeking to counter its colonial history. The oppressed people whose work operated monuments like Mount Vernon, the White House and Monticello have been illuminated in recent years by exhibits, oral history programs and other initiatives. Around the same period, scholars are gradually calling focus to the own slave-holding legacies of prominent historical figures: from Thomas Jefferson to George Washington, William Clark of Lewis and Clark, Francis Scott Key, and other Founding Fathers. Several American leaders have been complicit in maintaining the plantation system. Many, like Washington, Jefferson, James Madison, and Aaron Burr, supposedly sexually abused enslaved women working in their households and had often overlooked biracial families.

Although the Emancipation Proclamation was issued by Abraham Lincoln on January 1, 1863, it took two and a half years for the decree to be fully enacted. June 19, 1865—the day Union Gen. Gordon Granger informed Galveston, Texas enslaved individuals that they were officially free. According to NMAAHC this was America's "second day of independence." Originally kept primarily in Texas, the freed slaves dispersed across the World as they escaped from the South. This has been dubbed the Great Migration.

At the start of the social revolution in 1916, 90 percent of African Americans already resided in the South. According to Isabel Wilkerson in 2016, "[they were] kept hostage by the modern bondage of sharecropping and debt peonage and separated from the rest of the world." Sharecropping was a system in which formerly enslaved people became tenant farmers and lived in "converted" slave cabins. This was the impetus for the 1919 Elaine Massacre, which found white soldiers collaborating with local vigilantes to kill at least 200 shareholders who have the courage to criticize their small salaries.

Conditions outside of the Deep South were more favorable than those within the region. However, according to Wilkerson, the "hostility and hierarchies that fed the Southern caste system" remained major obstacles for African American migrants in all parts of the country. Low-paid jobs, redlining, restrictive housing covenants, and rampant discrimination have limited opportunities, creating inequality that would ultimately give rise to the movement for civil rights." The Great Migration has been the first major move the servant class of the country has ever taken without requesting, "explained Wilkerson.

> *It was about an organization for a person who was refused it and whose only choice was geography. Given the fear that they had suffered, the nation whose prosperity was created by their ancestors' unpaid labor was able to resolve it was an act of confidence.*

RACISM AFTER THE CIVIL RIGHTS MOVEMENT

The Civil Rights Movement was a struggle in the 1950s and 1960s for African Americans to gain equal representation under U.S. legislation. This was a battle for social reform. The Civil War had formally ended slavery, but it did not bring an end to injustice against African Americans. They continued to suffer the crippling consequences of racism, particularly in the South. By the middle of the 20th century, African Americans had racism and abuse toward them more than necessary. Together with many Caucasians, they mobilized and started an unprecedented struggle for equality that spanned two decades.

WHAT ARE CIVIL RIGHTS?

They are the individual citizen's personal rights, which are upheld by law in most countries. The American Civil Rights Movements is one of the most important campaigns in American history. It was a movement against racism and injustice that, in some way, affected every African American family in U.S and it had a lasting impact on later anti-racist movements. The Civil Rights Movement began in the 1950s when African Americans still lived in poverty. They suffered further degradation despite the abolition of slavery, under a system of racial segregation known as "Jim Crow" laws. Many southern states refused African Americans the freedom to register, to assemble, to speak. There was segregation of public travel, public bathrooms, and schools, with the poorest facilities reserved for African American men.

In Montgomery, Alabama the Civil Rights Movement began after a woman named Rosa Parks declined to offer up her seat on the bus to a white man. African Americans were required to pay for their bus fare, and then get on the bus through the back entrance. When all the front-facing "Whites Only" seats were full, whites had the right to demand that African Americans give up their seat in the next row. When she refused to move, Rosa Parks was dragged off the bus, arrested, and fined $10. That was the first time an African American individual was charged with breaking the segregation laws of the region. It was time to strike back, the African Americans decided to protest. A one-day bus boycott was initiated, but it was so effective that it. What began as a more sensitive treatment campaign became a demand for the complete abolition of segregation on the buses.

During the referendum year, many African Americans had to travel miles to work every day, and eight African American churches were bombarded by ignorant whites. However, this was the first major victory for the civil rights movement when the state of Alabama finally agreed to desegregate the buses. The churches were used to organize the campaign, which played an important role in the life of the African American community. Martin Luther King was one of the Ministers asked to lead the protest. He was the most popular figure of the civil rights movement.

SCHOOL SEGREGATION

In 1957, Little Rock in Arkansas was the site of the first conflict involving school desegregation. In the law courts, segregation in schools had been abolished. When nine African American teenagers tried to go to a school in Little Rock, racist whites physically prevented them. The government needed to send in troops to make sure the African American students could enter the school safely. The government has had to act for African Americans.

YOUNG PEOPLE & THE CIVIL RIGHTS MOVEMENT

Young people played an important role in the 1960s civil-rights campaigns. It all started when four African American students walked into a white-only canteen, refusing to leave until served. This was the beginning of the "sit-in" movement when young people entered lunch bars and demanded to be served. They would sit-in when they'd been refused. The attack represented a lot of revenue for bar owners. There were still more parties to take their position as police come to evict the demonstrators. Millions of young people were arrested, and many kicked out of school, but there were still sit-ins.

THE LEGACY

The civil rights campaign spanned over 25 years, arising out of its numerous anti-racist organizations and organizations. The movement to fight racism was not only about, it was also about fighting the poverty in which many African American families were forced to live. Such movements against racism and poverty are equally important today in America as ever.

The movement of Dr. Martin Luther King Jr. to secure fair access to affordable higher education for African American students persists more than 50 years after the enactment of the Civil Rights Act and George Wallace's 'stand in the schoolhouse entrance.' Last year, African American students, along with other minorities and white students, organized not only the legacy of injustice at their schools but also recent acts of racism on campus and a general state of inequality in higher education in protest. The country was made aware last year, from college marches to the Supreme Court, that much of the issues for which Dr. King battled are not the stuff of the past yet. There are many bright spots, however, such as higher college enrollment for African Americans and other minorities, successes in forcing universities to make necessary changes and the increasing influence of grassroots student movements.

An analysis below provides a brief overview of the important issues and events that have occurred in the past year, revealing that Dr. King's legacy is well-alive and that his work on many fronts is still unfinished.

STUDENT PROTESTS, RACISM ON CAMPUS AND BLACK LIVES MATTER

Student protests and activism in universities across the nation have increased in the last year. The Princeton sit-ins against racial injustice have looked like non-violent protest strategies. Even student protests such as the Million Student March, focusing on the debt of students, inevitably brought to the attention of the racism issues affecting university students in the Ivy League. The University of Missouri has "touched protests, hunger striking, the threat of a boycott of the football team and ... the resignation of the President of the university system and Chancellor of this [UM Columbia] campus" the New York Times, which reported on the misuse of the episodes racially charged such as swastikas on human waste walls.

In supporting Black Lives Matter, academics have been hitting campuses through a revolutionary campaign against juries who refused to prosecute young African American teenagers and African American people for killing. "After all, we live at the moment in history where the slogan 'Black Lives Matter,' which is not controversial, but appeared to be for so many whites, captured the attention of the nation. The reason is simple: The phrase briefly captures the danger of being African American in the U.S. today, "Princeton professor Keeanga-Yamahtta

Taylor wrote last year on why the movement resonated so strongly across university campuses.

Recognizing the broad reach of social media, this year, it was used by minority students to organize around issues of racism and injustice, with Twitter campaigns such as # BlackOnCampus opening up national debates on race and playing vital roles leading to university resignations. Unlike the social organizing landscape of the 1960s, now "In no time flat, a protest is going viral. You 're in an immediate news cycle with Instagram and Twitter, "UCLA's dean equity, diversity, and inclusion associate, Tyrone Howard, told the L.A. Times.

Student demonstrations lead to change at colleges, including Yale, whose chancellor vowed to establish a modern race and ethnicity learning center to study and fix bias and discrimination problems in higher education. And confronted with the national attention on university-level discrimination, growing faculty diversity became a significant topic, with John Hopkins, Brown, Harvard and several others pledging a rise in faculty leaders and academics from under-represented backgrounds, as well as further work focused on topics impacting diversity in education and around the World.

SUPREME COURT HEARS AFFIRMATIVE ACTION

For the second time in 2015, the Supreme Court heard Fisher v. The University of Texas questions affirmative action at university once again. For the future of affirmative action policies put in place to correct racial/ethnic imbalances in access to quality education, some of the remasks made by the justices were discouraging.

> *"[T]here are those who argue that it is not in the interests of African Americans to get them to the University of Texas where they are not doing well, rather than having them go to a less-advanced school, a ... slower track school where they are doing well," Justice Antonin Scalia said. "I'm also not pleased with the possibility that there might be fewer colleges in Texas. Perhaps she would have less [African Americans].*

His comments align with the "separate yet equal" claims that proponents of apartheid brought out in the past and may even surpass that. Judge Scalia did not seek to disguise fundamental differences that exist in higher education, proposing that maybe African Americans 'would' go-to 'slower colleges.' Martin Luther King, Jr.'s research aimed to guarantee equitable access to the best colleges for African Americans, whites and all those who desired to learn at such universities. His research has helped to illustrate the lack of funding and care in schools servicing significant African American populations, arguing for equal representation of these facilities and the young people attending them.

HIGHER COLLEGE ENROLLMENT, LOW GRADUATION RATES AND WAGE GAPS PERSIST

Adding to the Department of Education, "From 1976 to 2012, the number of Hispanic students grew from 4% to 15%, the number of Asian/Pacific Islander students grew from 2% to 6%, the percentage of African American students increased from 10% to 15% and the percentage of American Indian/Alaska Tribal students fell from 0.7% to 0.9%." However, graduation rates for minority groups still lag far behind the whites. What is more, major salary disparities exist in the workforce among African American and Hispanic graduates who graduate with bachelors or advanced degrees. And women are mostly absent from these classes from high-paying, high-demand jobs in STEM.

UNDOCUMENTED STUDENTS NO LONGER AN INVISIBLE CLASS

Dr. King tried to ensure that African Americans in their access to education and other aspects of daily life were no longer considered "second-class citizens." Today, undocumented students, an "invisible class" until recent years, have put Dr. King's teachings into practice, taking their own fate in the face of federal inaction, and working at the grassroots level to gain access to higher education and financial assistance.

Receiving help from several of today's most well-known faces, like Mark Zuckerberg and the United States Former First Lady Michelle Obama, these students gathered around the DREAM Act and obtained exposure to in-state tuition and financial aid, transferred word-of-mouth information on funding options and used technology to render access to college a reality for even more students and in Dr. King's spirit, in 2012, they were marching on Washington. Their actions have born some fruit, with many states and cities enacting their own rules to create a climate of inclusion for undocumented residents and to provide equal access for undocumented students to many of the benefits other students enjoy in their states and cities. Same the U.S. Last year the Department of Education published a training guide for schools to help meet the interests of illegal students in a more tenuous effort to offer resources for undocumented students.

The developments of last year and the big obstacles lead to 2016 as a significant year in progressing or unraveling the efforts of Dr. King and those who have worked to insure that students in all races and cultures have exposure to affordable higher education and a decent shot of a prosperous life that allows them to contribute productively to the nation they call home – the United States of America.

HYPOCRISY IN AMERICAN CULTURE

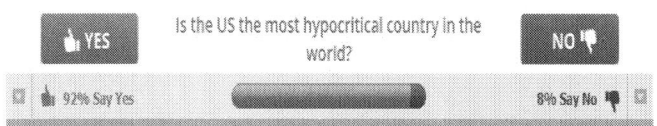

These days, watching American T.V. is like watching an exercise in hypocrisy. Consider this greeting first, Stay safe. Just like Take care, this is a uniquely American conception. Is it an order or a wish to stay safe? Is the person then saying the greeting to medical staff who have it within their remit to issue safety precautions? Finally, is there an underlying implication that the person being welcomed does not stay safe and must be chided as such?

Hypocrisy: the custom of pretending to have social values or principles that do not adhere to one's own actions. Americans do not enjoy getting picked out to be hypocrites. You know, they do not actually possess those people who pretend to have virtues, moral or religious beliefs, principles, etc., especially a person whose actions are contrary to the stated beliefs.

Americans know about the burning of Notre-Dame Cathedral on another world, so no less may worry about the destruction of churches in their own land by the son of a sheriff officer. Americans say that they care for worship houses, and some hide behind their religion to cover their racism. Americans will be conscious that churches are some of America's most divided locations, and Christian service hours are the most divided periods of the week. This week's media coverage highlighted how much more worthy of its attention are the White houses of worship.

As long as the unfavorable neighbors live on the other side of the city, you do not ask for anything (pull yourself up through the bootstraps). How one looks and from where they originate determines how (and if) they are being helped. We do not feed others the same way they feed their families; we don't treat other children the way they treat our own children and grandchildren, and within our borders, we don't love our neighbors. We are respectful of our neighbors. People are going to travel all over the World to purchase international orphans because it's simple and inexpensive, but not going to the hassle and red tape to adopt orphans in their own land.

Some love to tell the world that all men are created equal and that all life matters ... except that all life never mattered. Immigrants ought to learn when the terms in the Constitution, the Declaration of Freedom and the Bill of Rights arrive here, they are all phrases on paper, so there is no question about what liberty actually means. It is a dream for the U.S.A. Keyword: dream. We claim that we are free to go where we like, and this is the land of freedom ... except that is not the case for everyone. We see segregation and prejudice in our legal system, in our schools, in almost all city demographics. Government systems that do not match the words of the Constitution; forcing everyone who does not match the higher ideals to isolate themselves and/or segregate.

Americans want to claim they want to change all the wrongdoing. We are not going to do something. We sit in front of the screen and let wealthy commentators give us their thoughts on what we need to feel happier about what our loads will be in existence. We really do not want to get involved in the filthy mess the world has become around us. For all of it, many would not place their life on the line — except for their own convenience.

During all of this, we live in a country that is on fire; if you watch Al Jazeera or B.B.C. for a few hours, just like the rest of the country. People everywhere are fighting for their lives, though mainly where ethnic minorities live. The vestiges of colonialism on many of those nations are still wreaking havoc. In those places, the disenchanted and distressed people are tired, and they have nothing to lose. These angry people love their nations, so when they mistreat them, they are not scared to do something with their states, to include dying battling for reform. Worldwide, citizens are fighting for their life or internationally escaping oppression, violence, discrimination, and injustice. To name a few nations, just look at Sudan, the Gaza Strip/Palestine, Venezuela,

France, Yemen, and Colombia. People are fed up because they've got nothing to risk. There often comes a relentless abuse of our personal spaces or freedoms before the war. The motivator is the malaise. There has to be a war before any shift even happens. Change is hard, and change is hateful to those in power, especially when it does not benefit them.

Even Americans are not sleepy. We cannot get behind a single cause for something to get together in this country. American people have no problem destroying other nations with war, but they do not want anyone here to start issues on their own soil, keeping intact their pristine little places. Our enemies have found new ways to go to war with us. It has also been easy because technology and ease of access has made us open to our enemies. We are suffering from collective thought. Common sense is no longer common. When you take a long, honest look at Americans, we do not really advocate for anything, even while we do — we're not united together as a country of solidarity. Dividing and conquering us is easy because we have always been divided.

Americans love to tell other nations how to do democracy, but we are still a baby nation. We have not perfected the style of governance itself. We need to monitor ourselves and learn to sweep within our own front doors before our hypocrisy destroys another nation or person. We, the people, are America, and we are the one's that can change the narrative. It's time we Americans started keeping it real to each other, and to the World. We do not fool anybody – except ourselves.

EXPOSING THE HYPOCRISY OF AMERICA'S DEMOCRACY!

True Opposition Party aims to react to the atrocities of lynching carried out against persons of color daily in America. This chapter is informed by studies elucidating a contemporary understanding of race relations, racism, and the plight of the African American male in a 21st-century "post-racial" America.

By implication as concerning openness and the freedom to access knowledge, we take side with Facebook C.E.O., Mark Zuckerberg (albeit a capitalist), about why his company (Facebook) failed to block Trump's provocative comment in which he was trying to order the shooting of demonstrators to which Zuckerberg replied that-" I disagree strongly with how the President (Trump) talked about this, however, I think people should be able to see this for themselves, and eventually accountability for those in positions of authority will only happen when their discourse is scrutinized out in the open. " Zuckerberg has the freedom to have stood by his guns on the fact that streaming lives of horrific incidents in social media, especially meted out by law enforcement officers. Social media indeed gives the public a chance to play judge and jury in cases that could get swept under the carpet. Social networking also aims to minimize the risks of regimes running down from crime and criminology.

The latest tragedy in living in America was shortened, with George Floyd who died of an officer in Minneapolis lying on his neck — handcuffed; Ahmad Arbery, shot dead (February 23, 2020) by a former cop and his child while jogging; or Atatiana Jefferson (October 12, 2019), shot and killed by the police through the back window of her home; or Botham Jean (September 6, 2018), shot and killed on his couch by an off-duty officer who walked into Jean 's apartment; the recent attention surrounding the death of Breonna Taylor (March 13, 2020), a African American E.M.T. who was killed after officers forced their way inside her home to serve a search warrant. All have exposed the hypocrisy and fraudulence of America's democracy. Everything African American citizens are going through right now in America is witnessing the pandemic inside a pandemic – this is the twin ills of coronavirus and institutional injustice., causes a rather strong suspicion to America's " big and wonderful principles " in democracy.

AMERICA'S RACIST LEGACY

The continuation of fatal interactions with law enforcement involving unarmed individuals, especially African American males, is not accidental. Modern-day police brutality precursors against African Americans have roots in slavery. From 1877 to 1950, according to the Equal Justice Movement, more than 4,400 African American people, including women, and children, were lynched by white mobs. Some were shot, skinned, burnt alive, bludgeoned, and hanged from trees. Lynchings were often carried out by law enforcement officials and the Ku Klux Klan inside the scope of the structures of justice, on the courtroom lawns.

Historical narratives about the origins of American law enforcement during slavery show that squadrons made up of white volunteers were empowered to use vigilante tactics to enforce laws on African American people that were subjugated to slavery by then. Leaders of slave patrols might invade anybody's home with intimidation, irrespective of race or religion, on the assumption that they were sheltering people who had fled slavery. As Eastern Kentucky Gary Potter criminologist states, authorities will monitor a "dangerous class" of African Americans, refugees and the elderly. In the early 1900s, brutality and police abuse – particularly against citizens who were poor – became widespread.

In 1868, after the 14th amendment had been passed, the Black Codes were quickly defeated by providing equal rights to African American citizens, formerly slaves, by the Constitution. Since then, America has become a nation governed by the idea that it is centric to the rule of law, not rule by law-meaning, among many things, that the police are unable to take a life because they can, and no one is above the law. These "high and great principles which make America great," as a matter of law, do not apply to African Americans. In America, being African American is living a life booked by traumatic experiences. America's African American life is full of relentless vitriol and suffering deepened by horrific occurrences like several young African American men killed by police. Recorded historical accounts demonstrated how misconceptions, racisms, and divisive philosophies contributed to unjust policies and court decisions that fueled post-reconstruction racial brutality and resulted in America's dramatic increase in African American male incarceration. That is why, even during a pandemic which has disproportionately sickened and killed African Americans, the four officers who killed George Floyd felt free to do so anyway.

From this historical point of view, it is fair to say that the brutality against thousands of African American men who were lynched during the Civil War is a reference to the mob assaults and violent policing practices against African American communities being used today.

RACISM REVERBERATING TODAY

Criminal justice reports on race, class and crime in America show that African American people are mistaken for suspects on several occasions because of their skin color, and they pose considerable risks of inviting police disrespect, even physical harm. Even honest incident reporting is supposed to carry the risk of creating a victim's negative person. As one African American said,

"You're welcoming this huge system — which, honestly, does not like you — into your life by calling the cops. Sometimes you call, and it's not the help that comes. "That's why (Amy Cooper) cashed in on when she called the police on an innocent African American man, Christian Cooper (who was bird-watching in Central Park) and made up lies after flouting a dog-leashing rule in Central Park, New York City, on May 25, 2020. The white woman understood the implications of her position and her wealth-past and current in an effort to shame Christian Cooper by calling the police and referencing "African American" If she did not, she would not have said, "African American guy." By telling the police that she was being threatened by an "African American," the white woman made a split-second calculation in her determination to flout a dog-leashing rule to prove she was more important than Christian Cooper's right to protest.

The point is the U.S. government is morally unable to protect African Americans' lives and property. America's decades-old systemic sexism hasn't improved as much as it should. The prevalence in culturally segregated policing suggests the officers remain trapped in their historical discriminatory origins. Racism's origins in American police – first rooted decades earlier – have not yet been fully purged. This is why law enforcement reflects a history of increased disparity in the legal system and opposition to change among many African Americans. And as Khalil Gibran Muhammad, author of The Condemnation of Blackness, puts it, "for black Americans, the mechanism for racial surveillance and control has always been police."

These are the result of the American synonym for blackness with criminality. They are the product of White supremacist acts and decisions which converge and interlock to build the systemic Racism scaffolding. Despite the fact that the U.S. government has banned the usage of discriminatory laws at the state and municipal level, no change has been made in addressing the injustices that remain in African American and little has been done to encourage real social equity. Police are far more likely to murder persons of color than whites. What's more is that the vagrancy rules, defined as catch-all/stop-and-frisk – (a policing program that allows them broad authority to search, challenge, pull and detain too many poor African American and brown civilians at will) are heavily applied in today's America. For more than four hundred years, the United States has refused to handle people of African origin with decency, compassion, and empathy.

THE NEED FOR AFRICANS IN THE DIASPORA TO COME BACK TO THEIR HOMELAND:

Considering that living as an African American person in America has always been challenging as many are brutally marginalized and face daily inequalities, African American people must live in America and return to live in Africa. Living in Africa will put an end to the appalling hardships. African American people have endured in America for far too long. In Africa, unlike America, there are lower living costs, fresh food, ample land for residence, most of all farming, business ventures, freedom to be unapologetically themselves, and a sense of freedom not to have to think about race.

From this point of view, the Real Alternative Party calls on all African political rulers to commit free land and full citizenship rights to any African who wishes to repatriate to Africa as a return to his ancestral home. Real Alternative Party calls on all African political representatives to fulfill a moral duty to repatriate Africans in the diaspora completely should they wish to return, without subjecting them to the cumbersome processes that are visible in our laws surrounding the acquisition of nationality. Sending condolence messages and making gestures of remorse is a mockery of the situation African American people find themselves in. R.A.P. is persuaded that granting land and full citizenship rights to Africans in the diaspora is a sure way to provide the much-needed impetus to African growth, as Africans in the diaspora do not return empty-handed but with significant financial potential and scarce skills and expertise. Indeed, as Marcus Garvey steadfastly responded to the western Racism through his back – to – Africa's rallying call, "African descent people could establish a great independent nation in their ancient African homeland."

GEORGE FLOYD

Who happens to be George Floyd? The 'smooth giant' who has tried to turn his life around. The 46-year-old was known as "Big Floyd" to friends and had moved to Minneapolis to find work. The assassination of George Floyd has triggered demonstrations around the World, with protesters asking urgently for an end to police brutality. Mr. Floyd was an unarmed African American man who died as he told them "I can't breathe" after a Minneapolis police officer kneeled over his neck for more than eight minutes

After being released from jail, he transferred to Minneapolis and became recognized as a "smooth guy" who wanted to change his life around. The 46-year-old was born in North Carolina and resided in Houston, Texas, when he was younger but relocated to Minneapolis a few years ago to pursue jobs, according to Christopher Harris, his lifelong friend. He was known as "Major Floyd" to loved ones and was the parent of a six-year-old daughter living in Houston with former girlfriend, Roxie Washington. Ms. Washington told the Houston Chronicle that when they raised their baby, Gianna, together, he was a good parent. He also left a girlfriend behind, Courteney Ross, who said she was "heartbroken" about his death. "Waking up to see Minneapolis on fire this morning will be something which would devastate Floyd," she told the Star Tribune. "He loved the area. He came [from Houston] and lived here for the people and the opportunities."

Mr. Floyd was a talented athlete who excelled, particularly in school football and basketball. Donnell Cooper, one of Mr. Floyd's former classmates, said he had "a calm disposition with a friendly heart." He did not finish school, and he started making music with a hip-hop group called the Screwed Up Click, according to Ms. Washington. He quit the town for Minneapolis after having failed to find jobs in Houston. There, he served as a security guard at Latin American restaurant Conga Latin Bistro. In a Facebook post, Jessi Zendejas, a Conga client, said that Mr. Floyd "loved his hugs from his guests. [He] would be crazy if you didn't wait to meet him, as he loved to see people and to see everybody having fun," she added. Mr. Floyd's niece, Bridgett, said in a statement on a GoFundMe website that he should "give you the shirt off his back." His son, Oscar Smallwood, posted on Facebook: "The gentle giant has grown his wings, has not had the chance to tell that I love you!" Mr. Floyd was charged with armed robbery in a "home invasion" in 2007, according to court documents. He was sentenced to five years in jail in 2009 after a plea bargain.

THE DEATH OF GEORGE FLOYD, IN CONTEXT

In a horrific attack on race in America, the presence of influence and variation took on two events separated by 12 hours and 1200 miles. A white woman named Amy Cooper called 911 in New York City's Central Park on Monday morning and told the dispatcher she was being assaulted by an African-American individual. Christian Cooper, the guy she was concerned with, who is not a partnership, filmed the conversation on his camera. We were in the Ramble, a section of the park beloved by bird watchers, like Christian Cooper, and he only told her to leash her dog — something required in the field. Throughout the recording, Ms. Cooper tells Mr. Cooper before initiating the call that she is "going to inform them that there is an African-American guy threatening my life." Her needless presence of the alien race she hates appears only to invoke the ancient instinct to defend white womanhood from the challenges raised by African American people. To someone with a strong enough history or a relatively modern perception of the "If They See Us" show, this altercation 's location is part of the story: We remind ourselves of what happened in Central Park to five mostly African American and brown men accused falsely of rape of a white woman.

On Monday evening, a forty-six-year-old African American man called George Floyd died in Minneapolis, Minnesota, in a manner that illustrated the consequences that would have calls like the one made by Amy Cooper; George Floyd is how Christian Cooper would have been. (Amy Cooper apologizes for her action; she was also fired from her job, too.) (Police have not arrested or summoned in Central Park). Floyd was arrested by police responding to a shopkeeper 's call about someone trying to pass a potential counterfeit bill. Video surveillance shows a compliant man led away in handcuffs. Cell phone video later shows a white police officer kneeling for seven minutes on Floyd 's neck, despite onlookers protesting that his life is at risk. In an echo of Eric Garner's police killing in 2014, Floyd repeatedly says, "I can't breathe," and then, "I'm about to die." When the officer ultimately takes off his knee, Floyd 's body is limp and unresponsive. You can imagine a voice nearby shouting, "You just murdered him." Floyd was rushed to a hospital where he was declared to be deceased. A police statement said Floyd appeared to be in "medical distress," but did not mention his being pinned to the ground with the weight of a policeman compressing his airway.

Floyd 's death footage is tragic but not surprising; horrible but not uncommon, showing a form of event that is regularly reenacted in the U.S. It is both necessary and, at this point, pedestrian to observe that race mediates policing in this country. Hundreds of demonstrators, mostly sporting face masks to protect against covid-19 in Minneapolis on Tuesday, braved the pandemic to rally at the spot where Floyd died. Police vehicles were pelted with rocks outside of a neighboring precinct house, and officers responded by shooting tear gas, but within twenty-four hours after the video coming to light, the Minneapolis Police Department dismissed the officer who knelt on Floyd and three others on board. Mayor Jacob Frey tweeted "the right call," but here, the context is also important.

In November 2015, the police fired an older man named Jamar Clark, 24 years old, in response to news of a dispute in North Minneapolis between a man and a woman. Police and paramedics on the scene believed Clark had resisted arrest and attempted to seize an officer's gun; witnesses believed he had been bound and on the ground when the shot was fired. Amid his death, Clark's police division, led by Black Lives Matter, was amid more than two weeks of protests outside Minneapolis, demonstrating an effort to disrupt holiday shopping at the U.S. Mall and cascading scorn for African American voters who lost their election bid two years later to Mayor Betsy Hodges. In light of that history, Frey was unambiguous about the guilt of the police in the death of Floyd. "Being black is not meant to be a death penalty in America," he said Tuesday.

However, the larger issue is if the officials involved should suffer some legal repercussions. The Twin Cities area was an outsized part of the dialog over the use of force by police. The year after Clark 's death, a police officer in Falcon Heights, Minnesota, fatally shot Philando Castile, who was alarmed because Castile had a gun in his car, although he had identified himself as a licensed gun owner. (Castile 's girlfriend recorded the aftermath of her phone shooting.) In 2017, Justine Damond was fatally shot by a police officer who responded to her own call about a possible assault happening behind her home in Minneapolis. There were no charges brought against the officers in the death of Clark.

Jeronimo Yanez, the cop who murdered Castile, was dismissed from the force but cleared on prosecution for second-degree murder. Mohamed Noor, the officer who shot Damond, was convicted of murder in the third degree and manslaughter in the second degree and sentenced to twelve years and a half in prison. The case of Damond was atypical, both in that it required the deadly shooting of a white woman by a Somali origin African American cop, and that Damond was an Australian resident, which in the case created public demand for a prosecution. There were no charges filed against Officer Daniel Pantaleo in the death of Eric Garner on Staten Island, whose detention was also captured by a bystander on camera and has been frequently cited since the death of Floyd. (He was shot in 2019.) By a curious chance, "American Justice," a film depicting Pantaleo's mock trial for murder, has just been released.

The inquiry into the death of Floyd still occurs in the background of a continuing investigation into the death of Ahmaud Arbery, an African-American twenty-five-year-old who was fired in south-east Georgia while two people tried to execute the detention of a resident while a third filmed a video of the event. There is yet another investigation into the fatal police force in Louisville, Kentucky, where Breonna Taylor, an African-American E.M.T. twenty-six-year-old, was shot to death in her apartment by officers who were carrying out a drug raid at what her family said was the wrong address.

GEORGE FLOYD'S BROTHER CAME TO WASHINGTON TO SPEAK. BUT HIS POWER WAS IN THE SILENCES.

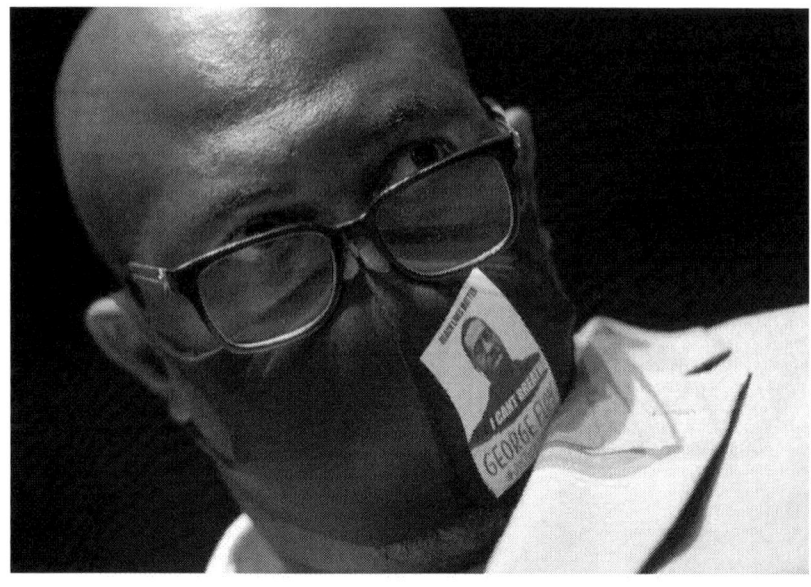

After looking at the death on video of his big brother, after grieving at several memorials, and after moaning at the funeral, which lasted for more than four hours on a Tuesday afternoon before the media, Philonise Floyd flew to Washington to testify. He walked into a political chasm: a hearing on police practices and racial profiling on Wednesday morning. Floyd was allotted five minutes in the opening hour of the hearing to speak about his older brother George Floyd, who died while being held down by Minneapolis police officers. But maybe what was conveyed in his silences, what occurred in the absences when he was seated alone behind his person witness seat, would survive.

He arrived at the hearing wearing an open-collar white shirt and a loose-fitting dove-gray suit. The lightness evoked the white suit he had worn the day before. His black mask bore a picture of his brother, a picture that is so familiar to the audience: George Floyd looks straight on; his eyes are alert and curious, but his expression is unsearchable. The picture on the mask is captioned as "I can't breathe," which was among the last words of George Floyd. Philonise Floyd does not put on a bow. These last few days, he hasn't been wearing one because he couldn't shake George's dying lament. "When he screamed, 'I can't breathe please,' I started wearing links. I didn't want to wear a tie anymore because I wanted to be able to breathe, "Floyd told the funeral in Houston. "I've been to memorials — no relation. I could've got one on. Still, I want revenge for my brother right now.

Floyd may still struggle to breathe freely, but he did not struggle to make himself heard as he sat facing the members of the House Judiciary Committee. He was the first of numerous witnesses, many of whom spoke distantly. But in person, Floyd was there, bringing into the room the full weight of his humanity. He explained how his uncle, even as he pleaded for his existence, called the police officers "sir" Floyd wasn't wading into the debate about "defunding the police." He simply asked lawmakers to "teach [police] what empathy and respect mean to treat people."

"He did not deserve to die over $20," Floyd said of his uncle, who was originally stopped after he was suspected by a merchant of selling a falsified payment. "I wonder: Is that what an African American guy is worth? Thanks to social distancing, the room was quiet and sparsely populated, as the lawmakers took his words in.

The president of the group, Jerrold Nadler (D-N.Y.), oversaw, restricting everyone within their minimal period and requiring both witnesses and participants to wear a mask, save for certain times when they shouted. Rep. Jim Jordan (R-Ohio) ignored that request and did not wear a suit jacket as usual. He has claimed that while he is adamant with being polite, he carries one, but a second encumbers his democratic pugilism. Jordan offered brief words of condolence and a fighting attitude. He quickly turned his attention to the property damage seen during the recent protests, after expressing sympathy for the Floyd family. And then he praised the leadership of President Trump in front of a man who could hardly get into a word of his own when the President called him to offer his condolence. Floyd's remarks were concise and concentrated.

But there were moments when he paused, and his hand swept over his bald head as if trying to wipe off the stress. For clarity, one fist softly hammered into the other — such a tender expression for a moment of furious emotions. There was no Floyd banging on tables or screaming out in a fury. Perhaps he simply felt too tired. Or maybe he understood that even now, in the minds of others, a righteously angry African American man is always too risky. His sniffles could be heard in the quiet between Floyd's words. His big brother missed the guy with the wide shoulders, the one he said looked up to. And he was tasked with stepping into the role of the head of the family, its strength. He 'd bear on. The lawyers spoke on and on, and so did the investigators.

The Republicans peered into their reading glasses, praising police officers, and labeling the officer in question as a rogue. They painted a picture of a destroyed country without police. The Democrats complained about African American lives being devalued and about systemic Racism. They expressed their support for effective justice, not their neglect of it. Representatives of the nation were yielding and talking and politicking — not to one another, but to the official record of the hearing.

Floyd was still listening late into the day. He removed his mask in his cool yet firm way to satisfy their queries. He shook his head in distress. He blinked hard until he could not hold back the tears, and with his broad, open hand, he wiped his eyes. Continued testimony. Yet Floyd pulled back on his mask, which told the audience that he was still unable to breathe.

COMBATING RACISM AND CHANGING THE WORLD

"Injustice for one is injustice for all."

– Dr. Martin Luther King, Jr.

Racism is a belief that there are specific (usually physical) classes of people that make them more or worse than others. Racist behavior can be not only overt, such as treating some people according to their race or color, but also covert, when society treats groups systematically according to some form of discriminatory judgment. The National Network to End Domestic Violence (NNEDV) is joining the global community to observe the International Day for the Elimination of Racial Discrimination on the 21st of March. During our battle to stop domestic abuse, we understand the value of addressing social inequality.

Racism is when an individual is viewed unfairly due to his race or culture. It may involve items like calling or missing names of individuals, and even refusing them service at a company or items like work opportunities. In the U.K., it is unethical to racism (treat differently) against someone regardless of their race. If you or anybody you meet faces racism, you should get support to avoid it.

WAYS TO HELP COMBAT RACISM

LEARN TO RECOGNIZE AND UNDERSTAND YOUR OWN PRIVILEGE.

One of the first steps to eliminate racial discrimination is learning to recognize your own privilege and understand that. Racial privilege plays in social, political, economic, and cultural contexts. There are two ways to start this complex process by checking your privilege and using your privilege to dismantle systemic racism. Yet race is just one privilege aspect. You may all be affected by ethnicity, class, orientation, skill status, socio-economic status, language and citizenship status. Using the rights that you must motivate us individually includes first becoming mindful of certain opportunities and understanding their ramifications.

EXAMINE YOUR OWN PREDISPOSITIONS AND CONSIDER WHERE THEY MAY HAVE ORIGINATED.

What messages did you obtain regarding people who are different from you as a kid? What was your neighborhood's racial and/or ethnic composition, education, or religious community? Why do you think it was so? These experiences generate and strengthen bias, stereotypes, and racism that can lead to discrimination.

Examining our own biases can help us work towards a level playing field for all.

DON'T TAKE OFFENSE.

Everybody is entitled, regardless of their nationality and race, to live happily and free of discrimination. This book gives information on what steps to take if somebody is racist towards you. The important part is getting away, remaining healthy and communicating to somebody you know. You do not have to take revenge or response. If, for example, you believe you have been unfairly discriminated against at work or by a company, you will find out your rights at Citizens Advice.

When anyone is biased against you, so your health is the most important issue. If you feel weak, stay with your trustworthy community of mates. You are not the one who creates problems. You made no mistake.

VALIDATE PEOPLE OF COLOR'S PERCEPTIONS AND EMOTIONS.

Another way to address the bias and recognize privilege is to support other people's experiences and engage in tough race and injustice conversations. In fear of "doing things backward," we should be reluctant to address inequality and racism. Take responsibility by discovering the forms of racism tends to influence our culture. Watching documentaries like 13th, for example, or reading books on how to stop racism. As authors, we learn about domestic violence through listening to domestic violence survivors. Similarly, speaking to persons of color is the only approach to recognize social inequality.

CHALLENGE THE IDEOLOGY OF THE COLORBLIND.

It is an omnipresent misconception that we exist in a "post-racial" world where citizens "don't see color." Perpetuating a "colorblind" mentality leads to racism in action. He did not say we could disregard race when Dr. Martin Luther King, Jr. mentioned his dream of living in a colorblind society. Racism cannot be eliminated without first recognizing race. Being "colorblind" denies a large part of the personality of a citizen and dismisses the actual injustices experienced by others as a consequence of ethnicity. To work together for equity and equality, we must see color.

KEEP THE FACTS.

Keep a diary of what is going on and save any messages or texts to show others how it affects you and what support you need. Before you seek justice, whatever information you may obtain would be of help to the prosecution.

CALL "JOKES" OR PRONOUNCEMENTS RACIST.

Let people know it is not all that racist comments. If you're not comfortable or feel uncertain about being confrontational, try breaking down their thinking process and asking questions. For instance, "that joke doesn't make me sense, could you explain it? "Or maybe you're joking, but that's what it says when you say that sort of stuff." Don't be shy to indulge in discussions with family ones, bosses, and peers. Microaggressions can manifest as racial remarks or comments reinforce and normalize inequalities and stereotypes. Know that doing nothing – or joking along – means you 're in agreement.

FIND OUT HOW YOUR COMPANY OR SCHOOL WORKS FOR PEOPLE OF COLOR TO EXPAND OPPORTUNITIES.

Systemic racism means that obstacles are imposed in the workplace and at school against people of color – including wealthy disparities, criminal justice and segregation in employment and housing. For instance, the African American Policy Forum (AAPF) revealed that a 12-year-old girl threatened felony charges in 2014 for writing "hello" on a locker room wall, in addition to being suspended from school. Their campaign, #BlackGirlsMatter, addresses issues within the education system of overpopulated and unprotected African American girls. Companies and schools need to tackle these issues and promote a culture of equity.

STAY SECURE ONLINE.

If you encounter harassment online, you can still submit it on any social networking sites, use the 'report violence' icon. Make sure you have safe privacy settings, too. The Safer Internet Center provides several tools with advice about how to guarantee that each of the social networking information is safe and confidential. Also, you can block individuals if they harass or bully you.

INVOLVE EVERYONE.

It is also learning about racism that is a major part of the war. You can start your school/youth group with an anti-racism project or newsletter or set up a discussion group to discuss relevant issues, and what you can do to help.

Don't Give Up!

You may not be able to deal with racism on your own, but we can all play a part. Challenging racism as you perceive something (without jeopardizing yourself) and exposing something helps make us know it is not true. Discuss what is happening with your teachers, young people, friends and/or family to help and support you.

Be Mindful Of Your Finance.

Take your wallet up a stand. Know the corporate practices you invest in, and the charities you donate to. Make an attempt to shop at independent, small businesses and return the money to the people who work in the city. The directory of local, minority-owned businesses in your area may be in your state or territory.

Adopt an approach that intersects in all aspects of your life. Remember, all forms of oppression are linked together. You cannot combat one type of inequality, then not battle others. Most domestic abuse perpetrators are still experiencing sexism, among other types of injustice. We ought to consider and back up the shared stories of survivors.

Try To Report It.

Racial crimes may be identified to Police by contacting the nearest police station, filling out an electronic application or calling the 911 number. The emergency number that you call has more information about what happens when you report an incident, what information you will be asked for and what may happen after the incident has been reported. When reporting the incident, you should ask for the reference number for the incident.

If you are having trouble saying or hearing English, you may ask the police to have a translator-they have to send you one. Remember: you do not have to be the ethnicity or religion that someone thought you are when they suggest anything to you or do it to make it a hate crime or accident.

SUPPORT FOR OTHER PEOPLE.

When you witness or experience anyone else being insensitive against someone else, you should help the person protect him. Just ask if they are all right, and let them know that what you saw was wrong can really help. When they decide to and want to be a victim, you might help them record it. It is also talking to third parties.

You may still criticize racism by saying you disagree with it in your mind whether you feel confident, and the situation means that it is safe to do so. Racism intervention provides a tool called Speak Up to help you realize how you can be what's considered a positive bystander, which ensures that anytime someone recognizes tension or inacceptable actions, they take measures that will create a change in a secure and respectful way.

HOW TO COMBAT RACISM AT WORK

No individual world can truly be rid of Racism, but human institutions, like sexism, should do a great amount to that inequality in the workforce. Few subjects in the social sciences have been exposed to more intensive and comprehensive study examination than discrimination, described as a discriminatory disposition toward an individual because of their participation in a specific category (e.g., gender, ethnicity, nationality and race), which is itself the focus of socially formed stereotypes.

Psychology tells us that we are all racist, because even in the presence of insufficient data and increased uncertainty, the same cognitive tools which enable the human mind to make rapid generalizations, lucid inferences and logical predictions are easily hijacked by our characters. In the name of self-justification, rationalization, and a very gratifying boost to our self-esteem, we would happily use an array of mental shortcuts to view the universe in a self-serving way, even though that includes belittling others. Paradoxically, by developing imagined in-groups that can live only in the juxtaposition of an almost hypothetical out-group, this bad practice literally helps one to communicate with others, a deep leverage bonds with others. That is our imagination 's power, those imaginary things can feel very real, taking over the real-world.

Even if our brains are pre-wired for harm, no one is born racist. As children, we are taught to be racist, by adults who help us codify the world in terms of good and evil, usually with good intentions. Thus, as our mind and intellect mature, we learn to be racist, dutifully absorb the dominant stereotypes in our culture, and do our bit to replicate and propagate them, so that they can be transmitted more widely. Although people are usually better at learning than without learning, we have the potential to change our attitudes and to adapt our behavior. After all, we aren't squirrels or fish, but a sophisticated thinking machine with unique flexibility and unrivaled adaptability in the kingdom of animals-and still technology. So, if we wanted to be a less racist version of ourselves, then there's no question we 're capable of it.

But do we want this? This is the critical question because there will never be any change-whether positive or negative-without intention and, in most cases, a true will to change. Trivial perceptions, including what you think about chocolate ice cream, are quick to alter, as you will go into your own experience and adapt your beliefs to control your habits and maximize your life for fun, like long-term enjoyment (which could entail less chocolate ice cream, even though you do like it). Deep societal beliefs, such as sexism, are even more difficult to alter as they are not merely based on urban traditions and commonly spread stories, they are the foundation of your social experience, the very prism by which you make sense of the universe. Only by doing the new is the path to unlearn this, but that would also allow us to destroy a conviction that helps us feel better for ourselves. Few techniques of self-deception are as successful and immobile as the propensity to raise our egos by taking down others.

So, clearly, if our hope is to live in a world without racism and bias, then we must manage our expectations. That is likely not going to be a human world. At the same time, there are also significant reasons to be hopeful, and the path to progress is not unknown, at least for those who want a more inclusive and ethical society. They may not have the remedy to eliminate discrimination, but they know very well that certain steps tend to reduce and regulate it, which explains why certain individuals, institutions, and communities are less racist than others.

The same is true of groups, of course: certain people are more open-minded, altruistic, and empathic, which makes them less discriminatory in general. The first and most impactful thing an organization can do to fight racism is to ensure that it ends up running it for such people. That is, placing people in control who are sincerely dedicated to diversity and equality, and who have the determination, bravery and commitment to fight for a new status quo. Change is more likely to occur top-down than bottom-up in any organization. Grassroots revolutions are now a black swan in culture but are much less prominent in businesses. Leadership is also a guiding force for change, and leaders have the ability to influence people's values and behavior. And, if you want an inclusive society, one in which justice, reverence and interest are harnessed and embraced, then build in the members an inclusive mentality that is only accomplished by first assigning inclusive members to the job. In the current climate, we expect these individuals to resemble morals rather than yuppy managers. Note that this is often difficult to achieve even in democratic societies, not least because leaders tend to reflect electoral values, and voters may not always want to prioritize fairness and inclusion. But the board and the qualified advisors nominate executive members who have fiduciary obligations and will be kept responsible for their decisions.

The second step that organizations should have to take because they are involved in combating racism, or even some form of racism, is to sanction it. Culture always includes both explicit and implicit rules to govern its members' interactions, and it is the job of the organization to instill a culture of civility, respect, and kindness. This does not happen by box-ticking tweets, spontaneous police or fragmented gestures, but by a concerted, long-term and systemic initiative aimed at developing an egalitarian community in which groups not only feel "tolerated," but are genuinely respected and celebrated; in which citizens are viewed as persons rather than collective categories; and in which administrators and staff are praised for improving themselves. The community still develops, whatever it might be. It's not stagnant but the continuous amount of what people do in a program, and not in it. Any H.R. activity-for example, job reviews, hiring actions, and leadership assignments-can demonstrate to staff that the organization has credibility (is their continuity in what leadership says and does?) or that it has become compromised by political and toxic powers. Unsurprisingly, nowadays the biggest distinction is not seen in what they think they like to be, but in who they truly are.

Let us note, eventually, that the only way to advance is incrementally to step by step. The first and most important step is to understand your problems because denial is an enemy of progress number one. Organizations, like men, ought to check in the mirror and see who they are and what they don't want. The next step is, to be honest about who you want to really be and why. Trying to be somebody else, or copying what your opponents are doing, may not actually work for you. You need to find a better way of being yourself, rather than a better way of being someone. This means understanding your potential and the specific constraints and opportunities of the context within which you are. It involves calculating where you are now, forcing yourself through a day a little harder. Development is not a straight line, yet neither does the cycle stop.

HOW TO TEACH YOUR CHILDREN ABOUT RACISM

There is no question: it can be sensible to talk about race, and yes, even a little messy. Choosing whether to speak about race with your kids or not is a choice many parents, particularly those of color, do not have. Some kids may eventually learn about it by addressing racism in their daily lives. Bias incidents darken our news feeds in an era rife with division and escalates our anxiety. We asked leading experts how parents might protect their children from an environment that appears hell-bent on hate — and steer them through.

Unfortunately, Americans are experiencing a disgusting golden age celebrating all sorts of hate — racism, anti-Semitism, sexism, transphobia ... Parents worry about exposing their children from early childhood, distorting their views about diversity and inclusion. But here is some hopeful news: Before it is too late, you can counter the insidious reach of hate. We have asked experts in child psychology and the fight against Racism to provide guidance on putting malevolent events and beliefs into context, dispelling misunderstandings of children and empowering your children to be forces for good.

AGES 0 TO 6

Your task in these early years is to lay the positive groundwork, tackling hate by cultivating its opposite — compassion and tolerance. Thankfully your child has a head start: an innocent indifference to what distinguishes people. Children are very aware of the ways in which we differ but are not born to identify people with a particular race, gender or ethnicity.

The hope is that children who grow up in ethnically, socio-economic, or otherwise diverse communities will get acceptance baked into their worldview. It's not sure, but research shows it helps. Nonetheless, researchers recommend taking the world home if you are not used to people who look like it or behave like it: learn other cultures together by dining and viewing their movies. Exhort the instructor of your child to integrate multiculturalism into their curriculum. If you are bilingual, speak your mother tongue, or encourage your child to study another language.

A 2014 research at the University of Chicago showed that children who encounter several languages in their everyday lives are more likely to embrace others whose language varies from their own — which is a turning stone toward a wider tolerance nature.

You do not have to preemptively teach the horrors of racism to a kid of this generation. ("I don't think I'd be sitting down with a 3-year-old and thinking, 'Let's speak about racism,'" Dr. Schonfeld says.) But if the need emerges for a discussion, provide one. "We had a surge of attacks from bombings at Jewish cultural centers in 2017. You 'd see very small children evacuating from those facilities on the news. Sure, they knew something was wrong, and they were scared. And of course, you 'd like to speak to them about it.

This might sound unlikely, but the trick to promoting anti-racism in children is to maintain the spectrum and vocabulary manageable. "You would say something like, 'the person who does this must be very angry,'" says Dr. Schonfeld. But, in solving problems, we use our words. Silence is worse because the interaction sounds strange. Imagine you 're four years old, and you realize that Dad's staring at his phone, he's upset, and people are worried, but no one is telling you what's making him upset.

AGES 6 TO 8

Talking about hate is clearly better at this era, but do not assume it must be a very structured discussion. "Families talk about these issues all the time, but they do not know," says Allison Briscoe-Smith, Ph.D., a Berkeley, California clinical psychologist who specializes in child trauma and studying how children understand race. "People are really sensitive to what is acceptable and not reasonable. This is a good platform to tackle inequality.

Let your child lead you. Children of this era will express their emotions, and it is not – and should not – be important for them to initiate the discussion. Ask her how she knows what she hears. What do people on the playground say? What did she watch on T.V.? You can maintain the conversation at the right level — reassurance, honesty, and detail.

The key is to not overdo it. Be transparent, short, and as truthful as you may if you have a conscientious desire to tone down. Here will never happen what happens at the garlic festival, stop it. An empty promise sounds a lot like disregard, and if you're afraid about the events, you won't take them seriously. Tell her instead what you know for sure: you love her and adults work to keep her safe.

Children may have a peculiar, simplistic vision of the universe and can question anything that sounds odd yet important for their comprehension. As I said to my daughter of eight that Osama bin Laden was dead, she told me, "Where is his body?" It was a strange question, but what they really want to know cannot be trivialized. You may also learn that your child misunderstood part of what happened, possibly anxiously overwhelming the event. But there's a calming answer for any concern like "We can't go to Walmart; people get shot there." You could say, "I know why you thought it, but that's a very unusual event, and it's unlikely to happen again."

Ages 9 To 11

Child psychologists say helping adolescents handle traumatic incidents in modern years has been a somewhat difficult challenge. The omnipresence of technology gives children unprecedented exposure to information that they do not mature. "Once the advice was: turn off the television; do not permit children to have access to death pictures," said Dr. Briscoe-Smith. "But they've got mobile by 9 or 10. They can see it there, and they'll see it on hundreds of other cameras. We will also help them grasp what they are seeing and experiencing.

Even with security, upsetting news and abhorrent views will reach your child. Your child. My children tell me that kids in their school taunt Hispanic children about I.C.E.: 'You run faster, I.C.E. is going to grab you.' Evidence indicates that ethnic discrimination has intensified over the past three years. So, I ask, 'What do you mean by people at school, what does your phone say? This kind of inquiry is needed, especially if you have a child who is not coming naturally. "You can't rely on your children to bring trouble with you," Spiegler says. You must ask. You must know. Rumors spread in school and online like wildfire. Help them bridge the gaps. 'I'm not positive it was in Minnesota that direction,' you might tell, before describing how it happened.

Your child will often begin to get negative views from others he meets and loves at this point. Grandma shares a homophobic meme; at the BBQ, the friend goes talking on the need for a boundary wall. Your child may be confused, rightly: he cares for him, but his beliefs are different from that of his family. Address these differences. Stay neutral with your language. We respect Grandma, so we talk about her differently. She has agreed, but we have come to specific assumptions.

TWEENS AND TEENS

As children prepare to leave their childhood, they build their sense of identity and lay the foundation for their becoming. As we noticed in the press, this era may be a source of reference. Many children, even most of them, choose a life of acceptance, compassion and respect for others. Others are going to travel a darker road.

Speak out if you see your child participating in biased thoughts or hatred speech online or in life – and yes, even children from socially conscious, justice-oriented parents do so. Dr. Briscoe-Smith says, "Adolescents try to develop their own beliefs. "You say, 'We're not on that page—so what do you think? "Note that young adults sometimes struggle to understand the entire meaning of issues. "Over-simplifications are stereotypes," says Spiegler. "When your kid falls into them, it's your job to help make his thoughts interesting and to see complexities he does not understand." They continue to leave the dialogue accessible to make it plain that they do not support assumptions or racism. 'I don't think about that, so I do not agree that anything you do is polite.' Or: 'I used to think about that, to instead I read X or heard Y.' Just if it does not appear, it is listening to everything you suggest.

Other children may feel compelled to act in the face of these distressing problems. This is a strong impulse, and it should be supported by parents. "It must not mean the beginning of a foundation. It could be, "I'll do one sort of thing today," or even, "I've not been well asleep because I'm frustrated, so I'll make sure I 'm getting more sleep. Activism presents you with an organization, "Spiegler says. It's scary to see horrible things in the World, and if you feel that you help people feel like they are, you are encouraged.

Of course, none of this is convenient. You can stumble — these things are, after all, as complex as they are. But your strongest weapon here, like with all situations, is your intuition. It's special with any adult, child and circumstance. Yet we realize what our children can do and what they can achieve. It's all right for your child to see that you also react to these frightening times. If we don't indicate we 're upset, our children are going to feel odd if they're upset. We cannot teach coping because we believe that we do not really have to contend with it. Such discussions may not be easy; however, they are required. We need not only teach our children what is simple, we need to teach them what is essential.

CONCLUSION

The world is becoming no less diverse. People will never cease to marry, to engage with each other. Just by triggering a development mindset, can we truly think about ethnicity and racism? Parents at home really want to convince their children that humanity must come first. We will be all right to be weak, all right to be incorrect, and all right to contradict the facts we know. That is the path forward – frankly thinking about ethnicity and putting our history into account – to conquer racism one day in the future.

Promoting recognition of the negative effects of racism as unwieldy experiences, such as recent efforts to create a state-wide day of traumatic awareness, is an important step towards developing policies that are sensitive to the impact of these experiences on health, particularly in young children. Even though we are not the direct beneficiaries of open racism, everyone must contribute to a discussion for a healthier next generation to change the social context.

Now I realize what I did not as a child: **Racism is bad for the wellbeing of everyone.**

Do Not Go Yet; One Last Thing to Do
If you enjoyed this book or found it useful, I would be very grateful if you would post a short review on Amazon. Your support really does make a difference, and I read all the reviews personally so I can get your feedback and make this book even better.

Thanks again for your support!

Made in the USA
Middletown, DE
12 July 2020